About the Author

Asee N Silla loves simplicity in words and wishes to make them available to young and old alike. Since she was a young girl, she has been writing poetry but didn't value her writing as she felt everyone could write words. It was later in life that she found her voice and why she wrote in rhythm and repetition. Asee offers a creative rawness and openness for the readers to experience their own vulnerability through her words.

Forget/Remember

Asee N Silla

Forget/Remember

Vanguard Press

A CIP catalogue record for this title is available from the British Library.

ISBN 978-1-83671-045-5

Vanguard Press is an imprint of
Pegasus Elliot Mackenzie Publishers Ltd.
www.pegasuspublishers.com

First Published in 2025

Vanguard Press
Sheraton House Castle Park
Cambridge England

Printed & Bound in Great Britain

Dedication

To all the writers who believe words are expressed to unite, not separate.

FOREWORD

by Suzanne Hill, an award winning Canadian Visual Artist.

Forget/Remember is a long poem that follows the trajectory of a life. Asee N Silla, the author, has deliberately chosen accessible words and phrases that, in the simplest reading, outline one man's journey, past to present.

The language is straightforward, the phrasing spare, the words short and unambiguous. Is the rhythmic, repetitive flow indicative of the musical talent that is the creative foundation of this man's world? Are the chapters "movements" in the style of a symphony?

It's much more, however, than a fictional memoir.

The poem reads as a "narrated" stream of consciousness – mirroring the flow of interior thought, moving back and forth through past "real" events and observed responses to these events, looking at the emotions connected to these events – showing the ongoing impact of the past, often "forgotten", on changes and choices made in the course of a life. Considering the embedded (mostly unconscious) reasons for these decisions – perhaps triggering personal comparisons? Suggesting that conscious remembering may provide a certain amount of control over a life's journey.

A relationship brackets the start and finish of the poem. This seminal memory generates the potential transformation from passive "acceptance" and resentment to self-awareness and control...

Forget/Remember suggests that actively engaging the forgotten past – discovering underlying patterns of failure and success – becoming truly self-aware... is the beginning of a future.

Prelude

He remembered her
The girl at the bus stop
The one who saw his guitar
The girl who ran the coffee house
The girl who got him to play at the coffee house

It all came back
She came back
Where did she get lost
Where did he get lost
Lost to his memories
His memories of her

Was it the pills
The pills to numb his pain
Was it his wives
The wives who broke his heart
Was it the hate
The sorrow
The resentments that buried her memory

He remembered her now
He cried
She tried
She tried to remind him
She tried to jog his mind

He didn't see her
He didn't want to see her
He pushed her aside
He pushed her love aside
Only to find her
When her breath was gone
He found her

Section I

The Bus Stop

He wanted to remember
Remember her
How did he meet her
What was it about her

He had forgotten something
He wasn't sure
What was it

He remembered waiting for the bus
He was waiting with his guitar
He was going for a lesson
A guitar lesson

He had outgrown his father
In music
He had outgrown him

He knew
His father knew
He was taking lessons from someone else
He no longer needed his father

There she was
She came to him
She asked him about his guitar
Did he play the guitar
Was he any good

He didn't know what to say
He was too shy to answer
Too shy to speak about himself

She asked him if he could sing
Yes he said
Yes he could sing

She laughed
She said good
She was looking for guitar players
Guitar players for the coffee house

She explained
She ran a coffee house
A coffee house at school
At her high school
She needed people
People to play guitars
People to read poetry
People to sing

Was he interested
Interested in playing
Interested in playing at the coffee house
He smiled
Of course he was interested

The Coffee House

What else did he remember
The coffee house
He remembered playing
Playing at the coffee house
He remembered the dark room
The square boxes
The glass-coloured goblets turned into candles

He remembered the long curtains
Long curtains over windows
Curtains that blocked out the light
Curtains that created darkness
Darkness lit by candled goblets
While spotlights lit performers

How did she manage it
He wanted to know
How did she convince the school
Convince the teachers
Convince the principal
Convince the care staff
To run a coffee house

And yet she did it
Thirty or forty students
Sitting
Listening
Whispering
Drinking coffee

They sat in groups
Sat on the floor
On the floor around the black boxes
Faces lit by candled goblets
Watching performers
Performers in the spotlight

He played
He played his guitar
He sang his songs
Songs he wrote
Songs he wanted to share
Songs waiting to be shared

He shared his words
They listened
He shared his music
They heard
They liked his songs
They liked his words
They liked him

He was glad
He was on his own
No father
No sisters no brother
He was doing this on his own
He liked it
Doing things on his own

He looked at her
He saw her running here
Running there
Setting up
Setting up candles
Setting up coffee
Setting up tea
Setting up the next act

She was different
She was alone
She was doing this for others
She enjoyed doing this
She was alone

He stayed till the end
He stayed till everyone left
He stayed to help her
He helped her clean up
He helped her put things away
They put the drama class back
Gone was the coffee house

He walked her
He walked her home
In the late-night
He walked her home
She talked
She had never talked so much

He listened
He listened to her love of school
Love of swimming
Love of snorkelling

Snorkelling was key
Snorkelling was another world
He heard her
He heard what she saw
The rocks the weeds the fish

She imagined
She imaged she was a mermaid
A mermaid in a water world

They were near
They were near her home
They were a block from her home

She told him to leave
A block from her home
She told him to leave

She didn't want them to see
She didn't want her parents to see
To see she was with a boy
She didn't want him to know
To know she was breaking her word
Breaking her word with her parents

The Walk

He liked her
She listened
She had ideas
She understood things
She understood many things
With few words she understood

He wanted to spend time with her
She wanted to spend time with him
He was a boy
She was a girl
She wasn't allowed to be with a boy

Her family were new
They were new to this country
New to Canada
They didn't adapt
They kept their old ways
They wanted her to stay pure
They wanted her to marry well
She had to be pure to marry well

He wanted to go out
He wanted to go out with her
He wanted to take her to Hog's Back
Hog's Back was where his family went
His family paid regular visits to Hog's Back

She had never been to Hog's Back
Hog's Back had a waterfall
Hog's Back had a river
Hog's Back had trails along the river

She liked him
She wanted to go
How could she go
What could she say
What could she tell her parents

She didn't want to lie
She didn't want to fight with them
She wanted to obey them
She wanted them to love her

Her parents loved her
In their harsh way
They loved her
Their harshness was all they knew
To protect her
They had to be harsh

They didn't understand
They didn't understand the new world
They didn't understand its ways
They didn't understand its language
They came
They weren't prepared
They came anyway
To give their children a better life
They came

She got the courage
She didn't lie
She asked
She asked them
She asked if she could go for a walk
To go for a walk with a friend
She was walking with a friend at Hog's Back

Her father knew the place
Her father worked near there
Her father worked on a bridge near there
On a bridge that collapsed
A bridge that almost killed him

She asked them
She didn't lie
She didn't say which friend
She said friend
Friend was neither male nor female
Just a friend

They trusted her
They let her go for a walk
They let her walk at Hog's Back
She went for a walk at Hog's Back with a friend

He met her
Away from her house
He met her
Away from her parents
He met her

They walked
They walked to the river
They talked
They talked about their lives
They talked about their wants
They talked about their dreams

He loved math
He loved to make things
He loved making things that worked
He loved making things for others
He wanted to be a builder

She wanted to be a writer
She wanted to go to school
To go to university
To learn things
She loved learning

They looked at the falls
They heard the sound of the water
The sound of water splashing
The sound of water bouncing
Bouncing against the rocks
Bouncing against the boulders
Water drops bouncing against each other

The water was loud
The water was music
The water spoke to them
The water heard their dreams

A Magical Day

He liked her
He liked her a lot
He liked being with her
He liked how she knew him
She knew what he wanted
She knew who he was
He didn't have to explain himself to her

Was he in love
He didn't know
But she made him smile
She made him laugh
He was himself with her

He surprised her
With the fins
With the mask
He surprised her
At the beach
He surprised her

They were to swim
At Mooney's Bay
They would swim
At Mooney's Bay

They would tan
He didn't know
She didn't know
It was the last time
It was the last time they would see each other

She lied
To her parents she lied
For him she lied

She screamed for joy
She saw the fins
She saw the mask
She put on the mask the snorkel

She swam
With the fins mask snorkel she swam
She saw the world
The underwater world
The underwater world of fish rocks

He heard her
When she spoke he listened
He listened to her love
Her love of water
Her love of swimming
Her love of seeing the fish in their world

Together they swam
Together they saw the fish
Together they saw this world
This underwater world

They saw each other
They twirled around each other
Under this water world
They whirled

Their love grew
Under this water world
They knew
Under this water world
They found each other
The other
Each had been looking for

Though young
They knew
They knew love
They knew
How to share
How to care
How to listen
How to be together
They knew
If lost
They would find each other

If only they could stay
Stay in this world
In this underwater world
Forever
Fish in a bowl
Fish in this moment
Forever

It came to an end
The sun was setting
Darkness would fall
Darkness soon cast a shadow
A shadow on their moment
A moment that could not last
She would remember him
He would forget her

Section II

Music

His father loved music
His mother loved music
Music brought them together
Music married them
Music brought them children

They had four children
Two boys
Two girls
Each child more beautiful than the other
Each more talented than the other

The parents taught them
They taught them music
They taught them Orff

Parents taught them recorders
Children practised recorders
Every day they practised
After school they practised

Parents taught others
Taught others Orff
The parents became known
They became known for teaching Orff

Parents started a school
Started an Orff school
Teaching students
Orff made them money

They gave concerts
Students children gave concerts
They were known
They were known for their music
They were known for their children

The Child Prodigy

He was a genius
He would hear music
He would play it
He was a child prodigy
His father knew this
His father wanted this
Wanted to use this

His mother was proud
Proud of her blue-eyed wonder
Proud of her family
Proud of the music they made

Being Plucked

His father took him
From his class he took him
From his friends he took him
From his school he took him

He was good
He was too good
He was too good to stay at school
He was too good to learn at school

He would teach him
The father would teach him
The father would teach him music
The father would teach him music to travel

The father had a plan
They would travel
The family would travel the world
The family would make music travel
Around the country
Around the world
The family would make music

The family received money
The family received money from Canada Council
To make music travel
The family received money

He was fifteen
He wanted to stay
He wanted to learn
He wanted to be like the others

His father needed him
His father needed his skills
His father needed his talents
His father needed his music

He left
To be with his father he left
To be with his mother he left
To be with his brother sisters he left
He left to make music to travel

The Move

They left their home
They left to teach Orff
They left to teach far away

To New York they went
Parents four children
They went
To New York
To teach Orff

They were happy there
Their mother planted
She planted flowers
She planted herbs
She taught Orff
She revived the garden

The children played
They played their music
They played their recorders
They were good
Better than their parents
They were becoming better

They stayed
They made friends
With other children
They gave concerts
The family became known

Father was glad
Father got his dream
For a while he was happy
Happy with himself
Happy for his family

Father became aware
There was a war
There was a war in Viet Nam
They were in New York
Father was afraid

He feared for his children
He feared for the war
He feared for his family
He feared for their life in New York

Mother listened
Mother heard her husband's fear
She understood
She understood they had to leave
She understood they had to go
On an adventure they had to go
On an adventure far from war

Safe from war
To live a simple life
They had to go

They left New York
The family left New York
They sailed
Across the Atlantic they sailed
They landed
On an island they landed
On an island in Greece they landed

Greece

The family started
Started a life in Greece
Lived as others in Greece
Lived a simple life in Greece

He was brilliant
He was composing
With brother sisters
He was composing
Learning new works
Creating new works on the recorder

He loved Greece
He loved the water
He loved the music

He played
With his siblings he played
With the Greeks he played
With stray cats he played

Mother Father were strict
They had rules
They wanted the best
They wanted their children to be the best

Mornings were for music
Mornings were for schooling
Mornings were to be better
To play music better
To sing better
To compose better

Afternoons were for playing
For exploring
For digging
Digging for rocks
Digging for anything
Anything that caught their fancy

They led a simple life
With little
They had plenty
With little
They had joy
With little
They were happy

The Greeks were curious
Curious about these strangers
Curious about their ways
Curious about their music

The family played
They played their music
The Greeks heard

41

They heard their music
They wanted their music

The family made friends
With the neighbours
They made friends
With the shopkeepers
They made friends
They played music made friends

Mother Father began
They began training Greeks
Greek students came
Old young
The Greeks came

They shared their music
They shared their songs
They learnt new songs
They learnt Greek songs
They played Greek music
They played Greek music with the locals

Soon the strangers blended
Into the Greek life
The strangers blended
Into the festivals they blended
They blended
Their music with Greek music

Soon they gave concerts
Soon they had to leave
Too soon they had to leave

Section III

Wife I

They were back
Back from the time in Greece
Back to their home in Canada

They needed a place
A place to live
A place to call home
A place to practice their music
A place to continue their studies
A place to be normal
A place to lead a normal life
A normal life as family

They found a place
A place by the river
A beautiful place
Where they could swim
Where they could remember
Remember their time in Greece
Their small village
Their Greek friends

He loved their new home
Being close to the water
Close to the water to sketch
To sketch to draw
To sketch to think
To think about things he could make

When he was alone
He didn't have duties
He didn't have to listen
He didn't have to care
He didn't have to hear his father

By the water he would go
By the water he would sketch
By the water he made the images
Images that took shape
In his mind
In his world

It was there he met her
It was there she saw him
She was open
She was free
She was open with him
She made him feel big
She made him feel strong
She made him feel special

They walked
They talked
They lived next door to each other
He was surprised
He was glad
To live so close
So close to her

They saw each other
Every day they saw each other
Every day they played
Every day feelings grew

She was bold
She was bold with him
He was shy
She knew he was shy

The more he was shy
The bolder she became

He didn't know what this was
He didn't know who she was to him
But he knew
He knew he wanted her
He knew he wanted her to be bold with him
He knew he had to have her
They finally kissed

He had to go away
With his family he had to go
Away to play music
Away to different cities
Away to different concerts
Away to different listeners
Away to be heard
Away to be loved
To play their special music

He called her
When he was away
He called her
He called to hear her voice
He called to hear her laugh
He called to hear her boldness

Her voice made his heart sing
Her voice made his hair tingle
Her voice that made him feel
Feel like a man
What men feel
When alluring voices enter their bodies

He was growing restless
A restlessness he didn't understand
He wanted her
He wanted to have her as his own

The music was not enough
The family was not enough
The travelling was not enough
The applause was not enough
He wanted her

Did she want him
He didn't know
He needed to know
Did she feel the same

He gained courage
The courage to ask
The courage to seek the answer
The courage to say the words
The words to bring her to him

She said yes
She said yes to his question
She said yes to his life
She said yes
She would be his wife

The union was set
The union was grand
The union brought their families together
The union was their stand

Her stand with him
His stand against his father
To be like his father
To be without his father
To have his own family like his father

They became united
A feast day for all
A feast day to enjoy
A feast for a union that would fall

It did not take long
For them to lose their way
The happy couple
They had had their day

Something was wrong
She was not happy
She wouldn't say
He was happy
With her he would stay
Still she went away

His father was glad
Glad to have his son
Glad his son had not won
Glad his son would not leave
Leave the group for his wife

He was back
Back to sing with the group
To sing with the family
The family he did not have

He went with them
He went with the family to sing
He went with the family to bring
Much music much fame many riches
They could claim

They travelled far
To distant lands
To newfound freedoms
To newfound glams

They met with musicians
Young and old
Some quite famous
Some quite bold

They grew
They became better
The children didn't need the parents
The children didn't need their lessons
The children outgrew their music
Still they went on

It was their father
Who told them what to do
Who told them what to sing
Who told them where to stay
How to live
How not to have their day

They stayed to play
They stayed to sing
They stayed to do
As they were told
For a while they would not be bold

He was not happy
He felt alone
He lost his wife
The first he'd known
The first to love him in such a sweet way
He wanted such a love
A love that would stay

Wife II

They were home again
From their tour
From their applause
From their shows
From people who taught them
Taught them more
Gave them respect
The respect they were yearning

They were good
They were very good
They were known throughout the land
Throughout the country they had shows
Throughout the country tickets were sold

Their father was proud
This is what he had done
These were his children
To complete what he had begun

The son was not happy
He wanted a mate
He wanted more than music to play
He wanted a home
Children too
He wanted something other
Than the life his father wanted

He met her
At a concert he met her
She was a singer
An angel's voice she had
A voice that would blend
Blend well with the family

His father was happy
He knew his son's needs
His father was happy
He knew his son's wants
His father was happy
To keep his son with him
His father was happy

His father liked her
For she could sing
His father liked her
She was good for his son
His father liked her
No more to be done

She brought him joy
This girl who could sing
She brought him laughter
This girl with the smile
She brought him peace
This musical delight
She brought him joy
For once his father was right

He married her
His second wife
He married her
She brought him life
She gave him laughter
Time to play
She brought him comfort
Love happiness each day

She joined their music
She was part of their song
She was part of the tour
For her husband she went along

His father was glad
His father was right
His father did what it took
To keep their music alive

The father kept the family singing
He kept his family near
The father needed them close to him
For losing them he did fear

For a while they were happy
The son with his new wife
For a while they were happy
To have this new life
For a while they knew laughter
To play make sounds
For a while they stayed together
Nothing else to be found

They would travel play
Play music
His family his wife
On many small stages
In small towns to stay
They sang they played
To the audience's delight
They brought joy
To audiences they brought light

He was happy with her
With this new second wife
This woman who joined him
Joined him his family his life

His wife was all he needed
To help him stay strong
She brought him a daughter
Nothing could go wrong

This was new to him
He was now a father too
This was new to him
He didn't know if she would stay true

Would he be like his father
Telling everyone his game
Telling everyone his views
Telling everyone what to do

He didn't want to be his father
He didn't want this for his wife
He didn't want this for his child
He didn't want this for this new-born life

His wife was not happy
To travel with them
His wife was not happy
To travel with this new-born child
His wife wanted something
Something stable
Something still
His wife wanted to be a good mother
To her daughter fulfil

He was torn in himself
Between father
Between wife
He wanted to please everyone
To do things right
His wife he loved his daughter too
He wanted to please his father
He wanted to be true

He chose
He chose to sing for a while
To sing to play to provide
To provide for his young family
To provide for his young child
He chose to be a father
A father to provide

He had to leave them
To travel to sing
He had to leave them
To travel to play
He had to leave them
To keep them afloat
He had to leave them
To keep them well
He had to leave them
To give them life
To make them happy
To fend off strife

He travelled with his father
His mother his siblings
He travelled with them
Till they could travel no more

His siblings were not happy
This life that was not theirs
His siblings were not happy
To fulfil their father's dream
His siblings were not happy
To sing their father's tune
His siblings were not happy
The family music was ruined

Family Music Ends

The family singing
Came to an end
What was he to do
All he knew was music
Skills to make money were few
He set himself up
As music for hire
He set himself up
So money he would acquire

He did well with this new gig
With music he composed
He did well with this new gig
His music became well-known

For his music
He won awards
Awards both near and far
HE
Became sought after
Much sought after for a while

His father was not happy
With his son's newfound fame
His father was not happy

For he could not claim
The fame for himself
For he was the one
The one who trained his son

This made him angry
This made him sad
He wanted his father to be glad
He wanted to share
Many things with him
To make him see
To make him hear
To make him love
The man he had become
Thanks to his father dear

To his father he reached out
As often as he could
To his father he reached out
As a successful son should

He longed so much
For his father's praise
He longed so much
For his father to hear
The songs he did compose

His father did not hear
His father did not praise
His father did not smile
For his son's good fortune
His father's doors were closed

Wife III

He was alone
For the first time in his life
He was alone
No wife no family to sing with
No one to call his own

She left him
The mother of his child
She left with their child
She left him
With his music with his thoughts

His musical family was silent
The siblings had had enough
Enough practice enough shows
Enough photos enough travel

Each wanted their own
Each had grown better
Better than their father
Better than their mother
They wanted their own
Their own life
Their own way
Their own time

Distance separated them
The parents were far
The siblings were far
His wife his child were far
He was alone

This was new
This was strange
Fear crept in
Raw silence engulfed him
It was hard to go home
Where emptiness echoed his fear
Where darkness gnawed
Crawled into his soul

He avoided
Avoided going home
Avoided the silence
Avoided the emptiness

He found a bar
Nearby he found a bar
A bar to make friends
A bar to hear stories
A bar to listen to others
A bar to call home

He became one
One with the bar
Friends with the owner
Friends with the drinkers
Friends with the servers

He met her there
At the bar
He met her
She was lovely
She was smart
He could talk to her
She could listen to him
He would talk to her
She would hear him

They became close
They became intimate
They shared each other's fears
They shared each other's aloneness

He brought her home
He brought her to his home
She stayed a night
She stayed another night
She stayed a week
She moved in with him

They drank
They talked
They shared each other
They knew each other
In all ways they knew each other

She was sad
She had a sad life
She cried
She cried a lot
He helped her
He helped her as he could
He knew her sadness
He felt her sadness
He was sad too

His child would visit
On weekends she came
On weekends she came for her dad
On weekends she stayed with him

His child didn't like her
His child wanted him
His child wanted her dad
His child wanted her dad for herself

The child left
They were alone
Again
In his home

They were alone
With their tears
With their love
With their fears

He liked her
She liked him
Sadness was present
Between them
Sadness was present
It would not go away

It was heavy
It weighed them down
There was no help
No one could help them
Together
The sadness became too dark
Together
The darkness broke their love

She left
He asked her to leave
She left
In tears she left
In tears he let her go

He was alone
Again
In his home
He was alone
Again

Wife IV

He had his work
He had his home
He had his music
He had his bar
He had his child

He liked his work
He liked the people
They liked his music
They liked what he did for them

The work was good
The work was different
There was always something new
New people to meet
New things to do
New ways to craft music
New ways to use his skills

He was happy
Though alone
He was happy

She started to work there
She started to work with him
Did he notice her
Did she notice him
Did she go after him
Did he go after her

It didn't matter
Soon they were together
Soon they spent time together
Soon they were an item

At work they were together
At play they were together
At meals they were together
They shared friends
They shared family

He liked her family
He liked her father
Her father was kind
Her father liked him
Her father liked everything about him

He liked her sister
He liked her sister's husband
He loved to watch them
He loved to watch the siblings
The stories they told
The closeness they had
The fun laughter they shared

They were a change
A change from his family
From his parents
From his siblings

Their love began
Their love grew
They travelled east
She had family in the east
She had uncles aunts in the east
She had people who loved her in the east

She had a child
She had a child the same age
She had a child the same age as his child
Their children were both girls
Their daughters played together
Their daughters liked each other

He liked being with them
He liked being with her
He liked being with her with her child
He liked her child being with his child

Time passed
They were happy
They were married
On a boat
During a cruise
They were married

She moved in
She moved in with him
She with daughter moved in with him
Soon his daughter moved in as well

This felt normal
This felt real
This felt like how it should be
This felt like the family he wanted

She was good to him
She made him feel good about himself
She made him feel special

The girls played well together
His child her child did many things together
He helped them with schoolwork
He brought them to dance classes
He taught them music
He taught them what he knew

He didn't know this
He didn't know this was what was missing
He didn't know this was the dream he wanted

Now he was his father
Now he had a family of his own
Now they made music together
Now they could grow
Grow to play
Grow to make music

He loved her
He loved her child
He loved their time together
Together at work
Together at play

She wanted changes
She wanted changes to the house
She wanted things bigger
A bigger bedroom
A bigger dining room
A swimming pool
A bigger patio

He did it
He did everything she wanted
He was happy to do this
He was happy to make her happy
He was happy to use his skills
To learn new things
To try things in different ways

His father wasn't happy
His father didn't want to know his family
His father didn't want to share time with his family

His father was disappointed in him
No matter what he did
His father was disappointed

The Tribe

He loved this wife
He loved her tribe
He loved how they were with each other
How they shared themselves
How they shared their stories
How they shared who they were for each other

The land made them
The land forged them
They survived the land
The rough terrain
The icy winds
The biting frost
The hard surface where plants were hard to grow

They survived this new found land
Surviving made them whole
Surviving made them real
Surviving gave them stories
Gave them laughter
Gave them song

Gave them stories to pass down to their children
To their children's children
To their children's children's children

The land held them
The land forged their spirit
The land gave them a sense of being
Who they were to each other
Who they were for themselves

He wanted this
To be part of them
To be part of this tribe
To be part of her family
He knew
He knew it couldn't be
He knew their stories were their stories
He had his own
He had his own stories to pass down

His stories were shaped by music
His stories were shaped by routine
His stories were shaped by a father
A father who had complete control
Complete control
Until he had none

Father Dies

His father was dying
The father who shaped him
The father who started his music
The father who set up his life

He was dying
He didn't feel a thing
He was numb
No tears were shed

He wanted to please his father
His father would not be pleased
He loved his father
His father ignored him

No matter what he did
What awards he received
His father was not pleased
His father did not care

This hurt
This hurt him deeply
This triggered the darkness
The darkness began to grow
Grow to take over everything

Everything he touched
Everything he saw
Everything he felt

The father died
The father who created the singing family
Died
The father who trained many
Died
The father who refused the Order of Canada
Died

No one came
No one came to his funeral
Though much sought-after
Father turned them away
Now they turned him away
What Father had done to son
He had done to others

The funeral was small
His wife his children few friends came
It was sad
All his efforts in vain
All the people he helped
No one came

The son understood
He understood why
He knew why no one came
Why no one paid their respects

The son would not cry
He could not cry
The hole was too big
The hole in his heart was too empty
He could not cry for his father

Something was different
Something was strange
Something had died
Love had gone away

The Darkness

The darkness came
The darkness grew stronger
No matter how he tried
The darkness grew

For a while he kept it at bay
For a while he continued to be himself
To love his girls
To love his wife
To love his newfound life

Things changed
His wife changed
They no longer worked together
They no longer played together

She worked in another office
She worked for the government
She became an important person
In the government
She had status
She had power to decide
She had to dress
She had to walk
Talk

To show her status
To be different
Different than him

He didn't know her
He didn't know who she was
He didn't know who she had become

She was not happy
She wanted him to change
She wanted him to be like them
Like the people she worked with
Like the people she talked with
Like the people she dressed for

They knew better
They ruled
They ruled the country
They knew better

He no longer was special
He no longer was important
No longer important to her
Her work was more important
Her new friends were more important
She no longer liked who he was to her

The darkness grew
The darkness took over his actions
The darkness took over his thoughts
The darkness made him do things he didn't want to do
He did things to his wife he didn't want to do

She still loved him
No matter what
Deep down she loved him
She saw the darkness
She saw what it did to him
Because of the darkness
He hurt her

Darkness took hold of him
The darkness that lurked
In his head
In his heart
In his soul
A darkness so deep
He didn't know it was there

The darkness lay buried
No one knew
He didn't know
He had planted seeds

Seeds of resistance
Seeds of regret
Seeds of rebellion
Like a mustard seed
So small
Yet grows to be so tall

The darkness grew
In bits pieces it took root
With each insult
It grew
With each put-down
It strengthened
With each rejection
It blackened

First it was his father
The father who robbed him
Robbed him of himself
The father who used his talents
Used him for his own fame
The father who wouldn't give him
The credit he deserved

Then it was his wives
One by one
They rejected him
One by one
They pushed him away
No matter how he tried
They didn't want him to stay

The darkness filled him
Took root in his heart
Squeezed out his soul
Burst out in anger
An anger he couldn't control

It was his last wife
She saw the darkness
She felt the anger

She knew
She knew what to do
She forced him
She forced him to confront the black

He listened
He listened to her
He listened to her pleas
He listened searched for help

On the phone
On the internet
Asking friends
He searched
He searched for help
Help from the darkness

He found help
The right person to help
The right person to shine light on the black
To guide him to his wife

Help came
With pills
With talk
He shared his darkness
In time the darkness left
The black became white

With help
His wife stayed
With the pill
His wife waited

She was not happy
The pill made him different
The pill made him numb
The pill took away the darkness
Took away his life
His love
His passions
The needs of a man
The need to be with a woman

Those needs were snuffed out
They were dulled
The pills dulled the senses
The pills dulled the heart
The pills dulled the passion
The pills dulled the man

He was not the same she said
He was not a man she said
He was not the man she married
He was just a shadow of himself

She was not happy
She did not like him
They did not play together
They did not make love together
She wanted more
He gave her less

The rift began
It became wider
They became silent
They spoke words
Words filled with anger
They did not listen
The pain would not let them
The pain would not let them hear each other

He was right
She was right
He was wrong
She was wrong

Words meant nothing
Words were empty
Words filled the rift with pain with sorry

He went into the darkness
She went into her closet
The darker he became
The more expensive her clothes

The daughters didn't like what they saw
They stayed in their rooms
Hiding crying
They stayed in their rooms

It was enough
She couldn't stay
She took her child
She took her clothes
She took the best of what they had
Of what they bought together

She left
With her daughter
She left
There was nothing he could do

He cried
Cried senselessly
He missed her
Tears were not enough
Tears did not bring her back

He was broken
His heart was broken
It ripped apart

He could no longer contain the darkness
He could no longer contain the tears
He could no longer contain the sorrow
The screams of pain would echo
Throughout the house
The screams of pain echoed

His child returned to her mother
He was alone
Again
He was alone

The divorce was nasty
The divorce hurt
He felt betrayed
The home he built
The walls he changed
The rooms he made bigger for her
She wanted it
She wanted it all

He fought
With tooth with nail he fought
With well-paid lawyers he fought
He could not lose his house
He would not lose his home
The home he bought
The home she moved into

It went on
The divorce went on
She paid for advice
She paid for her rights
She paid for what was hers

She paid too much
She got bad advice
She didn't get the house
The house stayed with him
He won the battle
The home stayed with him

Section IV

The Bar

He was alone
Again he was alone
He didn't like going home
To an empty house
A house with no laughter
A house with no talking
A house with no love
A house with an empty bed

He went back
Back to his bar
He stayed at the bar
To avoid going home
He stayed at the bar
He stayed to drink
He stayed to talk
He stayed to listen
To listen to their stories
The stories of people like him
Stories of people different than him
Stories to comfort him

Again he became one
One with the bar
One with the owner
One with the servers

Everyone knew him
Everyone liked him
He helped the owner
He helped the servers

He created music
He joined a band
Together they made music
Together they practised
Together they brought people
They brought people to the bar
The music brought people to the bar

He liked this
He liked being part of the band
He liked playing music
He liked watching people dance
People dancing to the music
People dancing to the music of the band

It filled the void
The emptiness
The darkness
It kept the darkness at bay

The Call

He was at work
He was at work when the call came
He knew her name
He talked
He shared
He shared his divorce

She was a client
She worked with his boss
She was easy to talk to

She listened
She shared
She shared her own story
She shared her own divorce

She had to go
She couldn't talk long
She wanted to continue
To continue sharing with him
She had other things to do
She needed the talk to end

She suggested a time
A time to continue sharing
A time to have coffee
A time to have coffee to talk

He agreed
He agreed to have coffee
He agreed to meet
A time was set

She came to his office
They had coffee at his office
She had never met him
She had never seen him

He was a voice
A voice at the other end
At the other end of the line
A voice who shared his life

She saw him
She knew
She knew it was him
Him from the past
Him from the coffee house
Him who swam with her
Him who bought her a mask
Who bought her fins
Fins to swim
Mask to breathe

She remembered him
He didn't remember her
He didn't remember the love
He didn't remember their kiss

She didn't say anything
She didn't bring up the memory
She wanted him to remember
To remember the past
To remember the love

The past was gone
Was the love gone
This was the present

She wanted him to know her
To know her now
To like her now
To love her now
To love the who she had become

She listened
She listened to his stories
To hear about his loves
His love of art
His love of music
The music he was creating
She liked him
She liked the who he had become

The Gallery

He liked her
He liked how she listened
He knew
He knew she liked him
He liked how she liked him
She made him feel special
She made him feel good
Good about himself
Good about his life

He invited her
He invited her to the gallery
To the gallery to see Gauguin
To see the Gauguin exhibit

They met
They met at the gallery
She arrived first
He was late
He apologised
He apologised for making her wait

They walked
They saw the art
They saw the paintings
They saw Gauguin's paintings

He talked
With knowledge
He saw what was good
What was mediocre
What he liked
What he didn't like

She listened
She agreed
She didn't know
She didn't know enough
Know enough to agree or disagree
She knew what she liked
She knew what moved her

The tour was over
There was a talk
A talk about Gauguin
She headed for the talk

He surprised her
He was hungry
He wanted to eat
Instead of the talk
He wanted to eat

They found a pub
An English pub
An English pub across from the gallery

He looked at the menu
He ordered his food
Steak with kidney pie
His favourite food

He liked its texture
He liked its smell
He liked his steak with kidney pie

He talked about his past
About his teens
About his time in Greece
A time he felt free
A time he had fun

He talked about his music
The family music
The practices
The tours

The meal was over
They said good-bye
He knew
He knew she liked him
He knew to keep his distance

Would he see her again
He didn't know
His life was full
He had his child
He had his music
He had his work
He had his fame

He didn't want anyone
He didn't trust anyone
He didn't trust himself
He didn't trust himself to love
He didn't trust love

He didn't remember her
She remembered him

The Christmas Party

They had a mutual friend
A friend who was his client
A client who became his friend

The friend was having a party
A Christmas party
A non-traditional Christmas party
To wear non-traditional Christmas clothes

The mutual friend invited him
The mutual friend invited her

She suggested they go
Go together to the party
He would pick her up
Together they went to the party

She wore pyjamas
Yellow pyjamas
Yellow pyjamas printed with bees
Yellow bee printed pyjamas
To a Christmas party

He saw her
He saw her pyjamas
He laughed
He helped her with her coat
He said something
He whispered
Love of my life

She heard this
She heard the whisper
She heard him say
Love of my life

She froze
Did he remember
Did he remember her
The girl from the coffee house
The snorkelling girl

She was afraid
Afraid to ask
Afraid to repeat his words

She didn't ask
He didn't repeat
They went to the party

He went in
He entered the party first
He entered alone
He entered without her

He saw her enter
He saw her
She entered after him
With her yellow pyjamas
He saw her enter

She was a hit
Everyone loved her pyjamas
Everyone laughed at the silliness
Everyone thought she was cute

At the party
He didn't speak to her
She didn't speak to him
She made jokes
She became the centre
The centre of attention

She did push-ups
On the floor she did push-ups
On the floor she puffed
On the floor she panted
She did twenty
Twenty push-ups
Everyone clapped

They left
They left the party
He drove her home
He hugged her goodbye
She laughed
He heard her laugh
He heard her cry out
He heard her say
When do we meet again

He liked being with her
She was becoming a friend
She was harmless
She made him laugh

Mondays
Let's meet Mondays he said
Mondays are harmless he thought

Mondays it is she said
One Monday
She cooks
Next Monday
He treats
Explore eating places

So it began
Mondays became their night
Mondays were harmless
Mondays didn't mean anything
Mondays were for friends

The Story

She had written a story
A story in rhythm
A story in repetition
She wanted him to write
To write music for the story

He read the story
He liked the story
The story surprised him

He agreed
He agreed to write music
Music for the story
They would work together
Work together on the story

They planned
They prepared applications
Applications for funding
Applications to Canada Council
To fund the story
To fund his music
To fund the music the story together

He liked being with her
She was a client
She would bring work
For him for his workplace
She would bring money

He knew how to please
Please to keep his distance
Work to not get involved

They spent time
Time to create videos
Time to apply
Time to know each other better

They wrote the application
The application for funding
The application wanted info
Information of past activities
Information of who they were

She wondered
These past activities
Would he remember
Remember the girl with the coffee house
What memories would be jarred
What memories would be stirred up

Nothing happened
No memories stirred up
No memories triggered
Nothing triggered him
He had forgotten
He had forgotten her
She remembered him

The story failed
The funding didn't come
Their music stayed silent

The Waterfall

He was at work
At work when she came
When she brought it
The pie
The steak with kidney pie

He was surprised
He didn't expect this
He wasn't interested in her
He didn't remember her
He didn't remember
The girl with the coffee house

She wanted him to remember
She knew
Even if she reminded him
He wouldn't remember

His anger
His resentments
His pain
His hurts
His pills
All these fogged his mind
All these fogged his heart
All these fogged his soul
He wouldn't remember

He was glad
He was glad to receive the gift
He was glad to have
This meal to eat

She was ready to leave
She hesitated
She wondered
She wanted some way
Some way to prick his memory

She asked
She got the nerve to ask
To ask him for a walk
To walk by the falls
The falls at Hogs' Back
The falls where they talked
The falls where they shared their future
Where they shared their future as teens

He was almost done
He was almost done with his work
If she would wait
They would go

They met in the parking lot
In two separate cars they went to the falls

He kept his distance
He knew the falls
He walked the falls
Many times with his family
He walked the falls

It was a regular place
A place where his family went
A place where they would rest
A place where they would rest from music from chores

She took off her shoes
He watched her take off her shoes
He watched her go down the rocks
Down to the stream
The stream at the end of the falls

He didn't go after her
He knew she was fine
He knew she could take care of herself
He knew no harm would come to her

He listened to her talk
He listened to her talk about another fall
Another fall in her birthplace
A fall she called la Rushna
A fall that was no more
A fall the rains swept away
A fall that was now a dry stream
Just rocks sand
No water

He heard her laughter
He heard her joy in her recall
The recall of the fall

He watched her
He watched her as she played
As she tipped her toes in the water
As she let the running waters
Cover her bare feet

He yelled out
You're such a girl he yelled out
You're such a girl who wants to play

He watched her
He watched her walk deeper into the water
He watched her come back
He knew it was time
It was time to go
It was time to return to their cars

He hugged her goodbye
He watched her walk to her car
He heard her yell
He heard her yell about a concert
About a concert in Montreal
About a concert they could go to

He knew
He knew she wanted him
He knew he didn't want to go there
He had had enough
He'd had enough romance
Enough love
Enough women
Enough to know
He didn't want anymore

He laughed as he got into his car
Let me surprise you he said
Let me surprise you was all he could muster

He received her email
The next day he received her email
She thanked him
He said she was such a girl
She thanked him for that

He had forgotten her
The girl with the coffee house
She remembered him

Mondays

He agreed
He agreed to see her Mondays
He agreed to eat with her Mondays
One Monday her meals
One Monday his treat

He liked being with her
She was fun
She made him laugh
She was not the same
She was not like other women

She didn't want anything from him
He was able to be himself
He teased her
He made fun of her

She didn't notice
She didn't care
She was herself

They walked
They walked along the canal
They walked by the river
They walked downtown
They walked in the mall

They talked
They talked about her
They talked about him
They talked about families
He mentioned his wives

They ate
They ate at cafes
They ate by the lake
They ate Italian
They ate Indian
They ate Canadian food

It was comfortable
Their walks
Their talks
Their meals
He was comfortable with her
She was comfortable with him

He hugged her
When they departed
He hugged her goodbye
Sometimes he kissed her on the cheek

He had forgotten her
She remembered him

The Fight

He was at the bar
At the bar drinking
At the bar talking
At the bar having his normal meal

He ate his meal
His meal of meatballs
Meatballs with ricotta cheese
He was alone
He didn't want to go home
He didn't want to eat alone
He ate at the bar

Two men were there
Two new men
Two new men drinking
Drinking while getting loud
The more they drank
The louder they got

The server warned them
She warned them to be calm
Warned them to not shout
Warned them to be quiet
Be quiet or leave

They did not like this
They didn't like to be scolded
They were not happy
To be scolded
Scolded by a young pretty server

One of them took her
Took the server aside
Yelled at her
Raised his hand
Raised his hand to hit her

He saw this
He left his meal
He left his meatballs to help
To help the server

He stopped the arm
He stopped the arm from hitting the server

His friend was not happy
The friend defended the man
The man hitting the server
The friend turned to him
The friend punched him
He punched the server's hero

He fell
The hero fell to the ground
He pushed himself up
He pushed himself up to strike back
To strike his hitter

His friend got behind him
He held the hero's arms
He held the hero's arms behind his back

The other man punched him
Once twice
He punched him a third time
The hero fell
To the floor he fell
Out cold he fell to the floor

The server looked at her abusers
She looked at them
She screamed
She left them
She left the hero on the floor

The abusers looked down
They looked down on the hero on the floor
They looked at each other

One of them kneeled down
He took out a little white bag
From his jacket he took out a bag
He slipped the bag into the pocket
Into the pocket of the jacket of the hero

They left
The abusers left
They left the hero on the floor
They left the hero on the floor with the bag
With the little white bag hidden in his jacket

The server came back
She came back with the owner
The owner saw him
The owner saw the hero
He shook him
He took a glass of water
He threw the glass of water on the hero

The hero moaned
The hero shook his head
His eyes opened
His eyes opened to see the owner
To see the server

They helped him to his feet
They helped him to his chair
They helped him to his meal

He ate
He finished his meal
They sent him home
The owner the server sent him home

They were glad
They were glad he rescued the server
They didn't want him to pay
To pay for his meal
They were glad he saved the server

The Arrest

They came
Early in the morning they came
Knocking on his door
Three officers were knocking on his door

They were tipped off
Someone called them
Someone said he had the powder

They had been watching him
For many days he had been watched
For many days they saw
They saw people
People on his yard by the road
People picking things up
People dropping things off

He went to the door
He didn't know who they were
He saw the uniforms
He saw the cars
He didn't know what they wanted

He let them in
Into his home he let them in
They had a warrant
They had a warrant to search his home

They searched his home
They found it
They found the bag with white powder
The bag with the white powder in his pocket
In his jacket pocket

He stood there
Stunned
He didn't know what to think
He didn't know what to say

He didn't say anything
He was given his rights
He remained silent

They put handcuffs on him
In his pyjamas they put handcuffs
In his pyjamas they put him in the car
In his pyjamas they drove him away

They put him in jail
He was given an orange suit
In jail
They made him wait
Wait for questioning

Wait for answers
Wait to explain himself
To explain where he got the drugs

The police asked
They asked about the drop-offs
Asked about the people
People dropping off drugs
Asked about the place
The place where drugs
Were dropped off
On his property

He was confused
He didn't know what they were saying
He didn't know anything about drugs
They kept asking
He kept denying

This went on
For hours this went on
He told them his routine
He told them about his music
He told them about his bar
He told them about the fight

He was charged
With possession
He was charged
They found the drugs on him

They kept him
For many hours they kept him
For many hours they asked
For many hours he was confused

He slept there
In the jail he slept
In the jail he slept with others
Others who were innocent
Others who were guilty
He didn't know
He didn't care
He wanted out
He wanted out of jail

Everyone knew
Knew of his arrest
He was famous
His arrest made him front-page news

They released him
The next morning
He was released
Released until his trial
Released under watch
To be watched

He needed a surety
A surety to stay with him
A surety to take him to trial

He asked his mother
His mother became his surety
He asked his daughter
She became his surety
He asked her
He trusted her
She became his surety

Each had to sign
To sign an agreement
An agreement to commit
Commit to keeping him in place
Commit
To bring him to trial

He called his work
They knew
He resigned
He resigned from his work
He resigned to spare them harm
He resigned to help them
Help them keep their good name

Sale of the House

It had to be done
It niggled at him
He knew
For a long time
He knew he had to do it

Sell the house
Remove the memories
Bury the past
Clean up the mess
The mess that had been mounting
The mess in his head
The mess in his heart
The mess in his house
The mess in his basement
The mess in his garage
The mess in his life

How did he let it happen
How did he let himself slip away
Slip away into nothing
Letting others control
Letting others tell him what to do
Letting others control his thoughts

He had his music
Music
The one thing
Was his music
People paid for his music
Use his music
Craft his music
Music made him

Where is the music now
Where in his house is the music
It was no longer present
The house scarred the music
He had to leave it
Time to sell

The house was sold
He had a few months before closing
Before he had to leave
A few months
To put his things in storage
To put his life in order

His case was brought to trial
The charges dropped
The men who planted the white powder were caught
This wasn't enough
Not enough
To bring back his good name
Not enough
To repair the damage

The media remembers the bad
Forgetting all the good
People never read
The corrections

Section V

The Note

He didn't know what to do
Did he love her
What did he feel for her
He liked her
He liked being with her
He liked how she liked him

He was afraid
He felt the pain the loss
The weakness of love
The weakness of wanting
Wanting someone
Wanting to be in control
Wanting to be in control of his weakness

He felt trapped
He wanted her
He wanted her friendship
He wanted to resist the pull
To resist the weakness
To resist not being in control

He read her note
He read her need to break free
To break free of him
To break free of a love she couldn't have

He didn't like the note
He didn't want to lose her
He liked what they had
He liked how they were
How they worked
How they talked
How they could agree to disagree
Only to agree again

He responded
He called her
He talked to her
He told her they were good together
He liked how they talked
He talked to her more than anyone else

He heard her silence
He heard the pause
He knew she cared
She cared for him
She cared for their work
She liked their time together

It was a long pause
It was a long silence
She said yes
She said yes to the friendship
She said yes to his terms

The Concert

He was annoyed
He was frustrated
What more did she want
She agreed to the friendship
She agreed to his terms
She agreed
To have him in her life
She agreed
To spend time with him
She agreed

Now this
This anger
This email
This dealing with her hurt

Yes he liked her as a friend
He treated her like all
Like all his best friends

Yes she paid
She paid for his ticket to the concert
Yes she paid
She paid for his meal
He would pay her back
He said he would pay her back
He forgot to pay her back

It was a good night
It was an enjoyable night
He enjoyed the concert
He enjoyed listening to his favourite pianist

What did it matter that he talked to someone
To the woman who sat beside him at the concert
What did it matter that he didn't speak to her
He spoke to her all the time
On the phone
Now that she was with him
Sitting on the other side of him
He didn't need to speak to her

He wanted to speak to the woman
He knew the woman
He wanted to know how he knew her
He knew her from work
Years before
He worked with her

What did it matter that he ignored her
He ignored his friend
The friend who bought the ticket

Now this
He read the email
She couldn't be his friend
She loved him too much
Too much to be a friend

That was it
The friendship was over
She was no longer there for his walks
For his talks

It was just as well
It was better this way
He didn't want a lover
He didn't want romance
He didn't want that entanglement

They always hurt
Love entanglements always hurt
She wasn't his type
He wasn't attracted
He didn't want her
He didn't need her

He had his mother
He had his daughter
He had all he needed in them
He had their love
He had their affection
It was enough
He didn't want more
He didn't need more

Section VI

Breaking Free

Finally he got away
Got away from the snow
From the sleet the cold the winds
He got away from the shovelling
The shivering
The clothing to stay warm

He went south
He went to a warm clime
To sands blue skies warm water
To a place he could swim
To drink
To speak freely
A place where no one knew him
Where he could give in to his urges
Urges that had been buried
Buried for a long time

He had been good
Good to live
Good to be free
Free of the stigma
Free of the pain
Free of the label given him

Because of the drugs
He was labelled
The drugs put him in jail
The drugs ruined his name
Everyone knew about the drugs
The drugs blackened his image

In this warm clime he could let go
He could let go of the pill
He could let go of the pill that numbed his urges
The pill that gave him peace
The pill that let him forget his anger

He was glad to give up his anger
He was glad to give up his urges
He was glad to give up his pill

Here
He was glad to be himself
To remember a self
A self-buried under pain
Under anger
Under shame

He gave up his pill
For a few days he let it go
For a few days he sought out warmth
Lay in the sun
Next to shimmering dark bodies
He lay in the sun

He slept
He slept with shimmering dark bodies
He felt their smooth dark skin
He felt their skin press against his
He remembered
For a few days
He let go
For a few days
He remembered

The Gravestone

He stared down at the gravestone
It had her photo
The photo he chose
The photo he chose for the website
The website they created
The website for the project

It was a lovely photo
It showed her smile
Her energy
The life energy came through
Her life came through
In everything
Her life came through
In her words
In her actions
The photo showed it all
The photo spoke her thoughts

He remembered her
It took a while
It took a while to see her
To see who she was
To see the girl he fell in love with many years ago
The girl he forgot
The girl who never forgot him

He loved her
He loved her more than he had loved anyone
He loved her
She knew him
Even when he didn't know himself
She knew him
She knew who he was
Who he would become
Before he knew
She knew

It took her death
For him to shed tears
It took her leaving
For him to feel his heart
For him to know love again

For this he was grateful
For this he was glad
For this his anger
His resentment
His fears
Disappeared

Love Her – Don't Love Her

She was dead
He knew she loved him
He knew she was devoted to him
He knew he wanted him
He knew he could not be with her

Did he love her
He wasn't sure
He liked being with her
He liked making her laugh
He liked teasing her
Getting her into a tizzy

He liked talking with her
Getting her views
Her ways of seeing the world
Seeing the world through purity
Through love
Through clear wonder

He didn't like that she listened
She listened to everyone anyone
She listened to everything
To people who didn't know
She trusted facts
Facts with no research

This bothered him
They would discuss
She would listen
She would listen to him
She would agree with him

She also agreed with others
She agreed with others
Who didn't agree with him
He didn't understand
He didn't understand that about her

He still liked being with her
She made him laugh
She made him feel good about himself

Why couldn't he love her
Why couldn't he want her
Want her like she wanted him

He wanted friendship
Didn't she know that
Why was she not happy with that
Why did she have to ruin that

He was happy
He was happy in his world
He had his mother
He had his daughter
He had his brother sister

He had his wives
He had his marriages
He had his divorces

No more
The tears
The pain
The break ups
He didn't want that
He'd had enough heartaches

Friendships are safe
No emotions
No pain
No hurts
No break ups
He just wanted to be friends

Why did she want more
Why did she want something
Something he couldn't give

He was loyal to her
Though he couldn't commit
He was faithful to her
As there was no one else
He trusted her
Though he couldn't be intimate

Could one be friends
Be friends
When one is in love
When the other is not

Does the urge to be close
To kiss
To squeeze
To be one with another
Does that ruin a friendship

Can men with women
Be friends
Can trust intimacy
Between these two
Remain still in friendship
Even when one is in love

She was dead now
Would he miss her
He didn't know

He bent down
Left her flowers
Flowers on her grave
Flowers he didn't give
Didn't give her when she was alive